More Time Pieces for Cello

VOLUME 1

Arranged by William Bruce & Tim Wells

ABRSM

MIX
Paper from responsible sources
FSC™ C109619
www.fsc.org

More Time Pieces for Cello
Volume 1

Published by ABRSM (Publishing) Ltd, a wholly owned subsidiary of ABRSM

Banaha

Trad. (Congolese)

Taivas on sininen ja valkoinen

Trad. (Finnish)

The Sky is Blue and White

AB 3535

1597   Come again, sweet love doth now invite

John Dowland
(1563–1626)

c.1600   Sellinger's Round

William Byrd
(c.1540–1623)

1689 Air

John Blow
(1649–1708)

1716 Sarabande l'unique

François Couperin
(1668–1733)

AB 3535

1742 Air
from the *Peasant Cantata*

Johann Sebastian Bach
(1685–1750)

1771 Moderato
from Trio Sonata No. 1

Domenico Gallo
(*c.*1730–*c.*1792–6)

1797 Poco adagio

from String Quartet Op. 76 No. 3 ('Emperor')

Joseph Haydn
(1732–1809)

Poco adagio e cantabile ♩ = 88

1842 Bella siccome un angelo

from *Don Pasquale*

Gaetano Donizetti
(1797–1848)

Andante ♩ = 66

AB 3535

1864 Berceuse

from *Dolly*, Op. 56

Gabriel Fauré
(1845–1924)

1874 Vltava

from *Má vlast*

Bedřich Smetana
(1824–1884)

1876 Rococo Theme

from *Variations on a Rococo Theme*, Op. 33

Pyotr Il'yich Tchaikovsky
(1840–1893)

1878 Slavonic Dance

Op. 46 No. 8

Antonín Dvořák
(1841–1904)

AB 3535

8

Roly Poly

Howard Bla[...]
(1938 -

© 1996 by Highbridge Music Ltd./Faber Music Ltd.

Hungarian Folksong

Ungarisches Volkslied   Chant populaire hongrois

Traditional
arr. A.G.

© 1996 by Faber Music Ltd.

Archangel's Lullaby

Wiegenlied des Erzengels   La berceuse de l'archange

Howard Blake
(1938 -   )

1880 Funiculì, funiculà

Luigi Denza
(1846–1922)

AB 3535

1884 Gavotte

from *The Holberg Suite*

Edvard Grieg
(1843–1907)

1939 The Peanut Vendor

Moises Simons
(1889–1945)

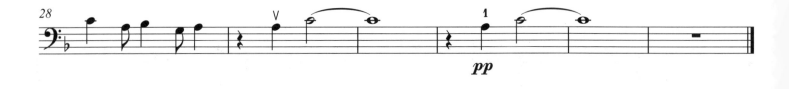

Published by Purple Patch Music under licence from the original publisher,
Termidor Musikverlag & Timba Records GmbH & Co KG

AB 3535

1963 The Pink Panther

Henry Mancini
(1924–1994)

1964 I wish I knew
(how it would feel to be free)

Billy Taylor
(b. 1921)

2008 Happy Places

Tim Wells
(b. 1977)

Music origination by Andrew Jones
Printed in England by Caligraving Ltd, Thetford, Norfolk

AB 3535

03:14